First Edition
Genuine Autographed Collectible

_____
Do you want me to sign it in ink or in lipstick?

Flunked History
Sitting All Day On Their Ass On College Grass
Dumb dee dee Dumb Dumb
Iranian Useful Idiots

Gift Card

Date:

To:

From:

Message:

Flunked History: Sitting All Day On Their Ass on College Grass

What Do Books Do?
BOOKS ARE POWERFUL!
Books Educate!
Books Enlighten!
Books Empower!
Books Emancipate!
Books Entertain!
Books Spring Eternal!
Books Drive Exploration!
Books Spark Evolution!
Books Ignite Revolution!

Sharon Esther Lampert

Centuries of Islamic Jihad Holy Wars "Allahu Akbar"

Flunked History: Sitting All Day On Their Ass on College Grass

Literature, Poetry, History, Jewish History, Sharon Esther Lampert

Flunked History
Sitting All Day On Their Ass On College Grass
Dumb dee dee Dumb Dumb

©2025 First Edition by Sharon Esther Lampert. All Rights Reserved. No part of this book may be used or reproduced in any manner whatsoever without written permission except in the case of brief quotations embodied in critical articles and reviews.

KADIMAH PRESS books may be purchased for education, business, or sales promotional use. Shop Global Bookstores

KADIMAH PRESS: GIFTS OF GENIUS
ISBN Hardcover: 979-8-3482-2802-6
ISBN Paperback: 979-8-3482-9125-9
ISBN e-book: 979-8-3482-9126-6
Library of Congress Catalog Card Number: 2025900090

Author Information:
FANS@SharonEstherLampert.com

Cover and Interior Book Design:
Creative Genius Sharon Esther Lampert

Publisher: PalmBeachBookPublisher.com
Phone: 917-767-5843
Email: Sharon@PalmBeachBookPublisher.com

To Order Book:
Ingram, 1 Ingram Blvd. La Vergne, TN 37086-3629
Phone: 615-793-5000
Fax orders: 615-287-6990

First Edition
Manufactured in the United States of America

Centuries of Islamic Jihad Holy Wars "Allahu Akbar"

Flunked History: Sitting All Day On Their Ass on College Grass

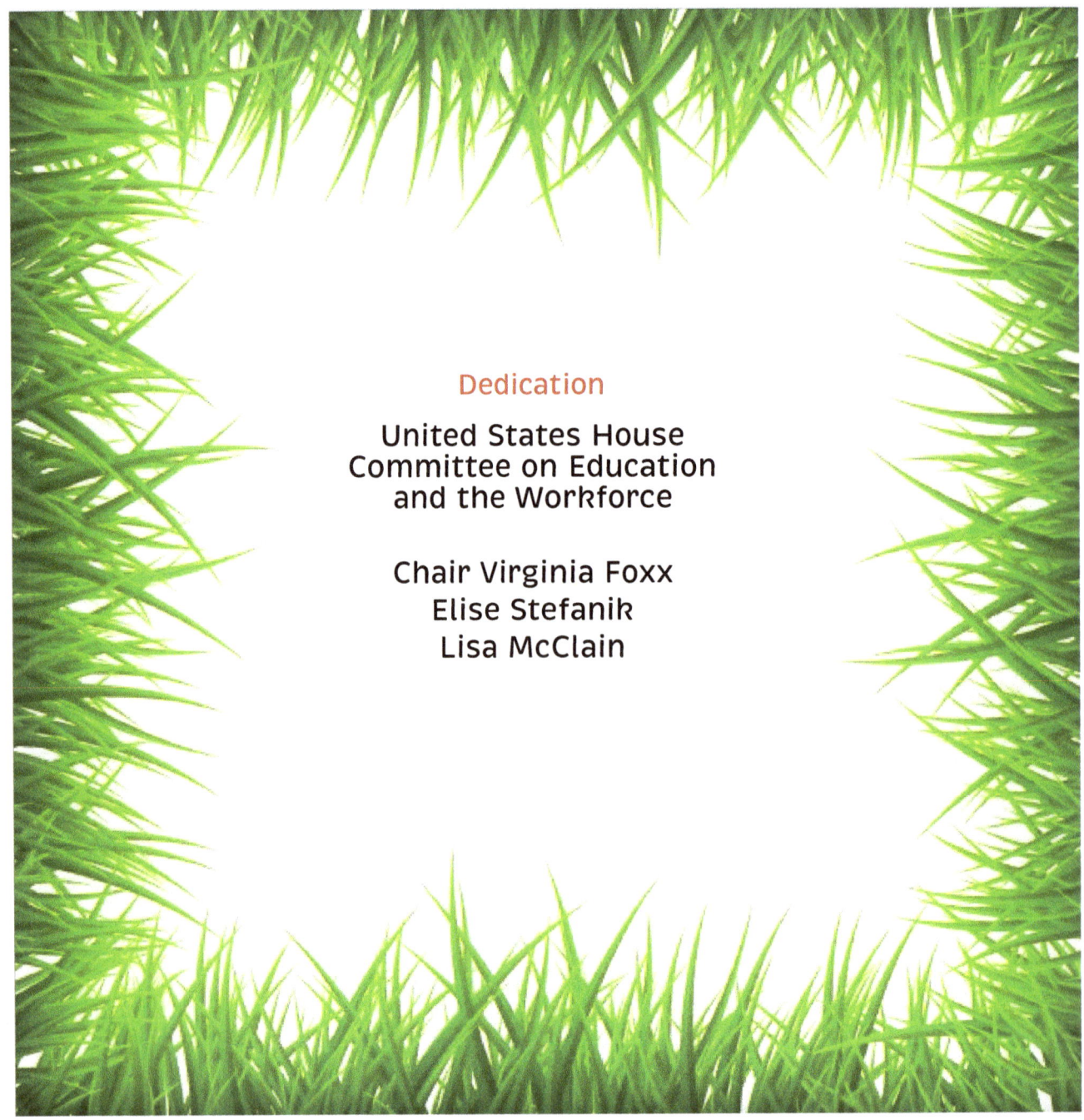

Dedication

United States House Committee on Education and the Workforce

Chair Virginia Foxx
Elise Stefanik
Lisa McClain

Centuries of Islamic Jihad Holy Wars "Allahu Akbar"

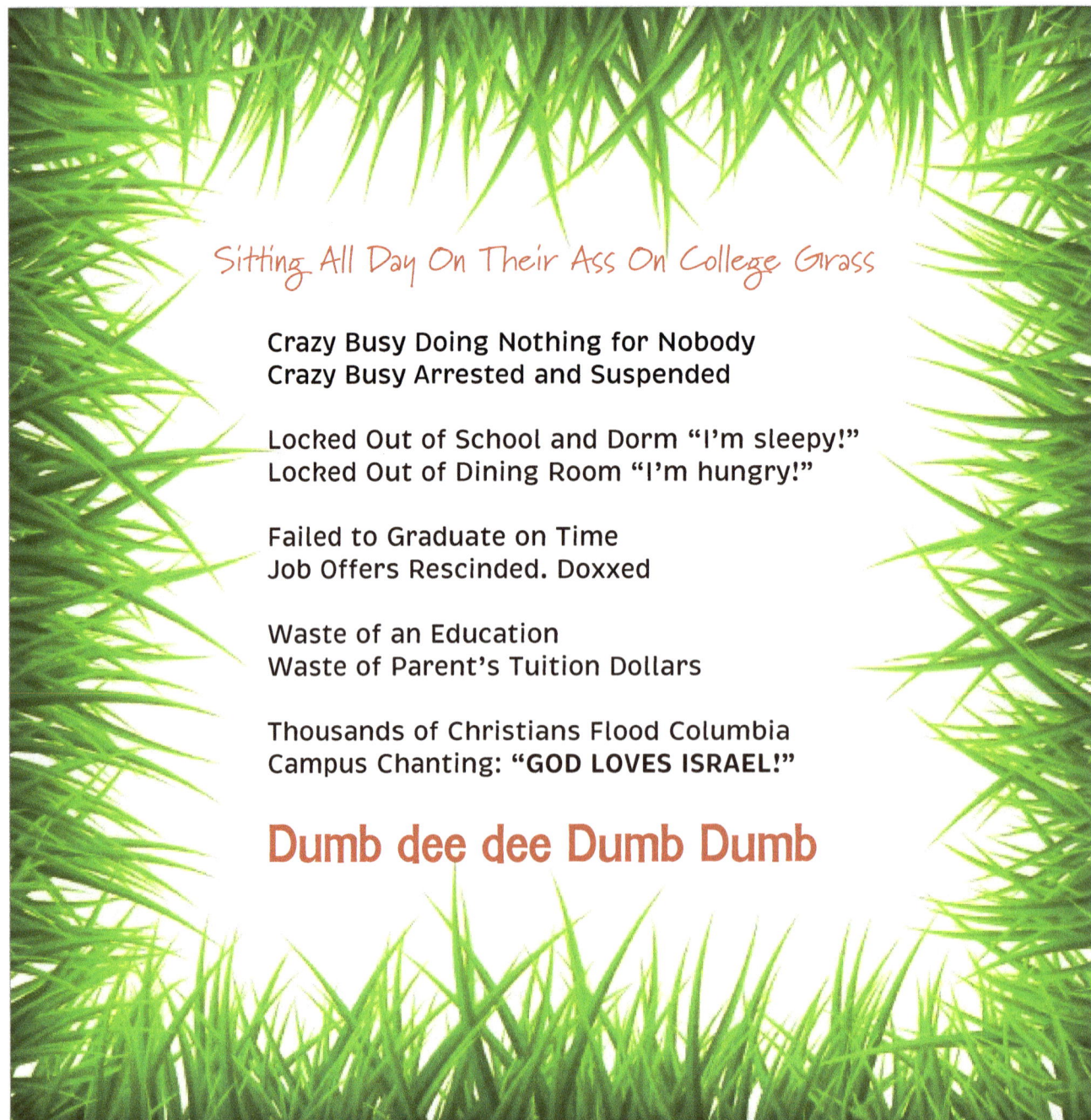

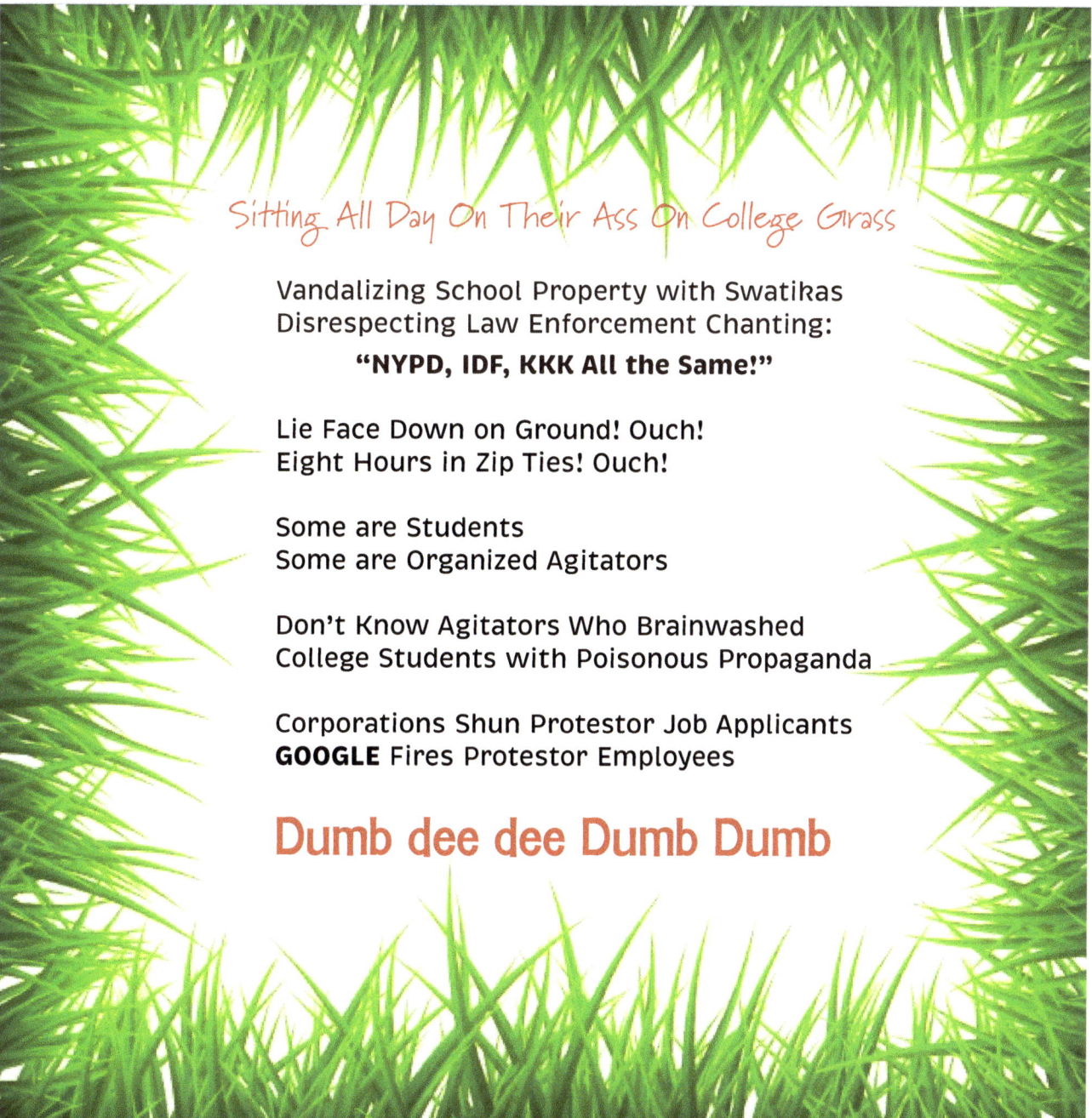

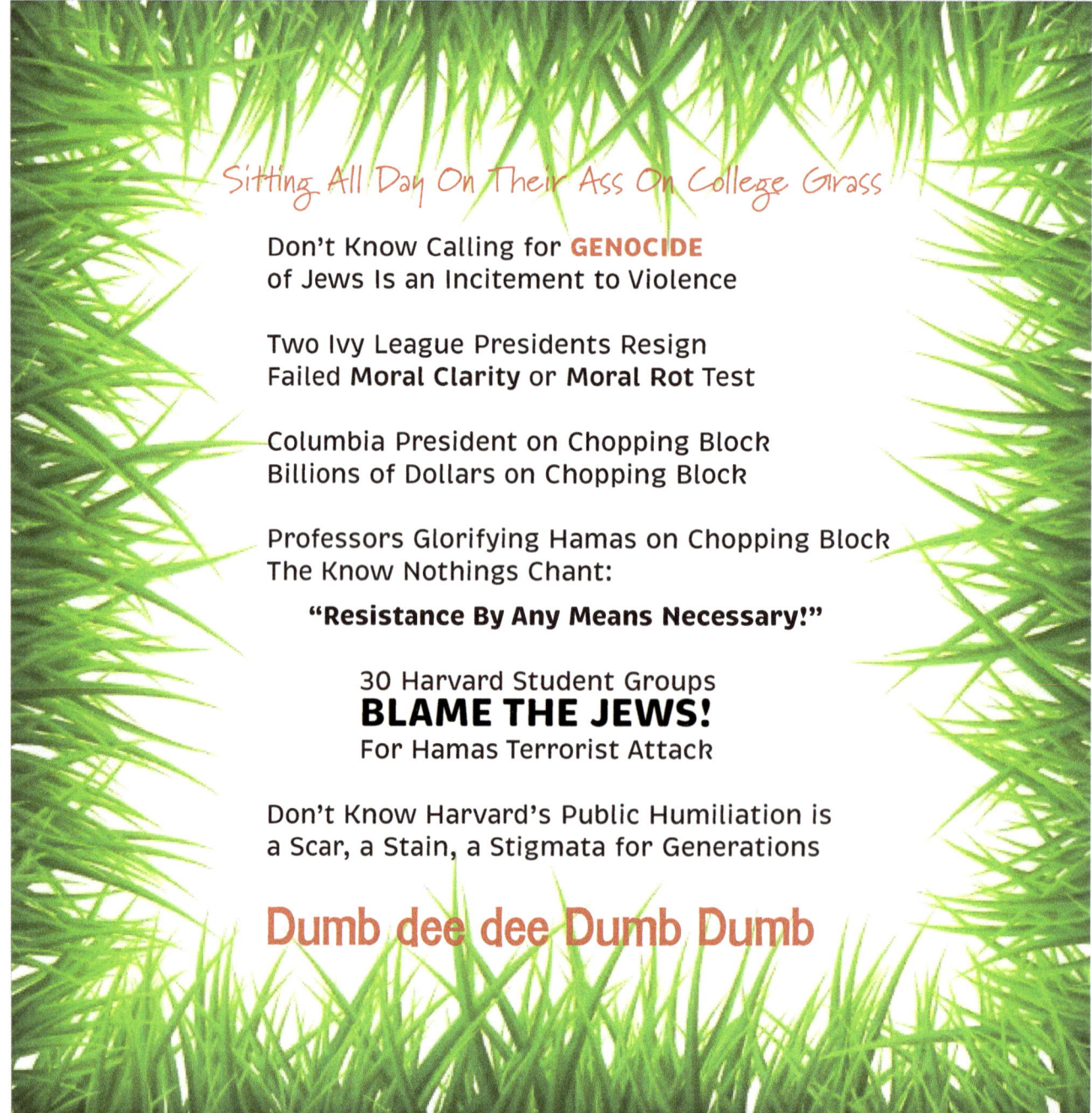

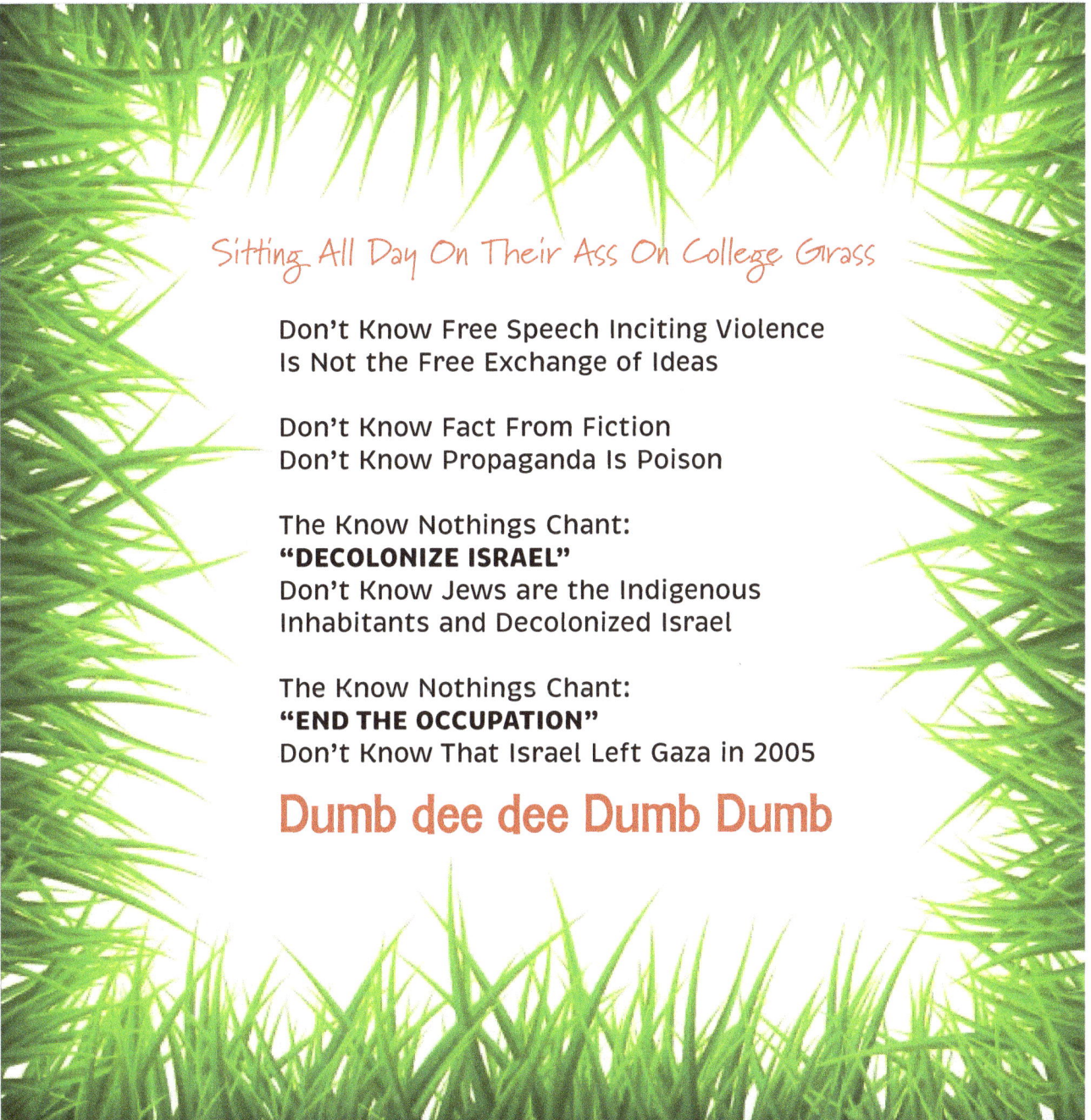

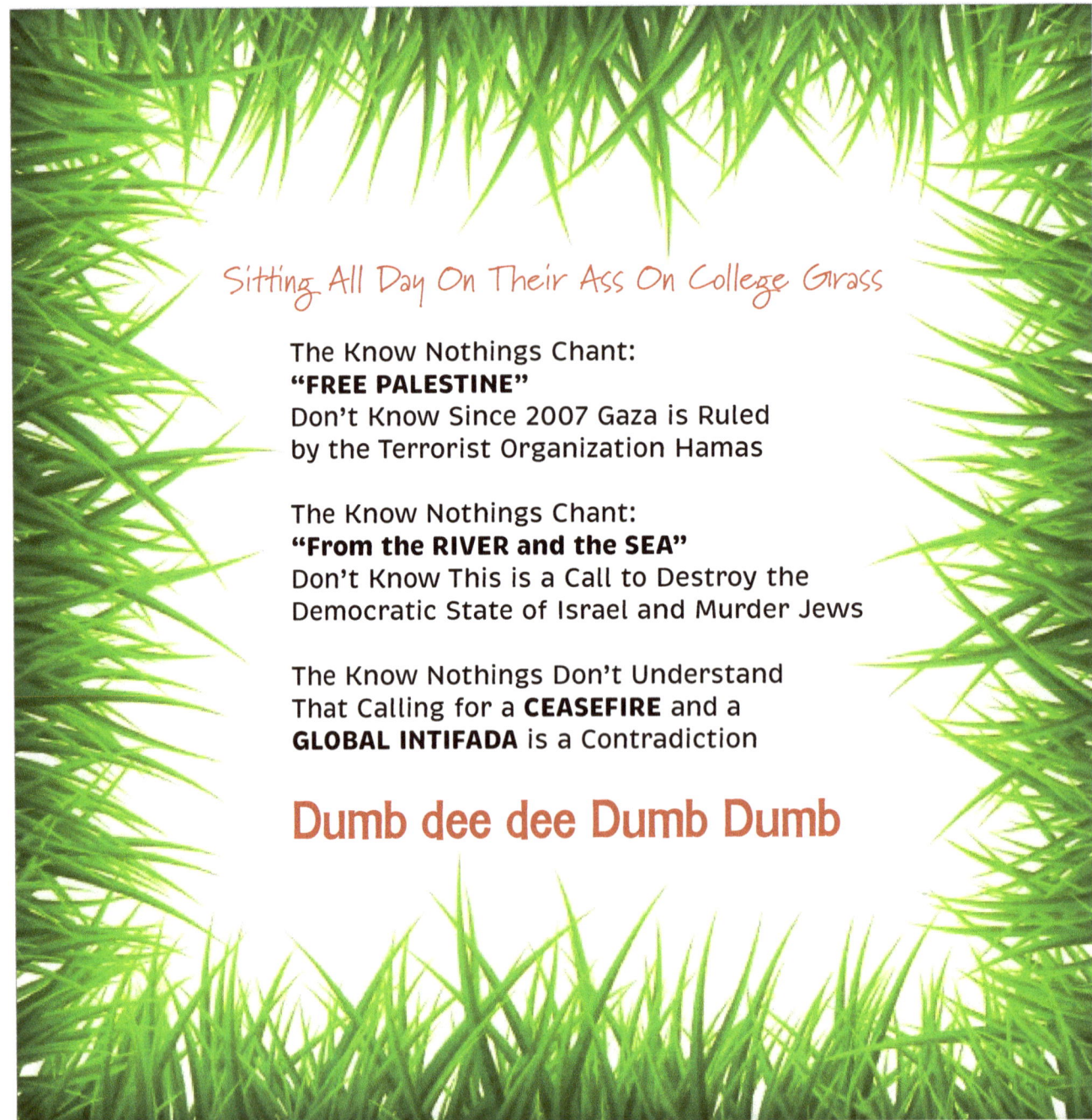

Flunked History: Sitting All Day On Their Ass on College Grass

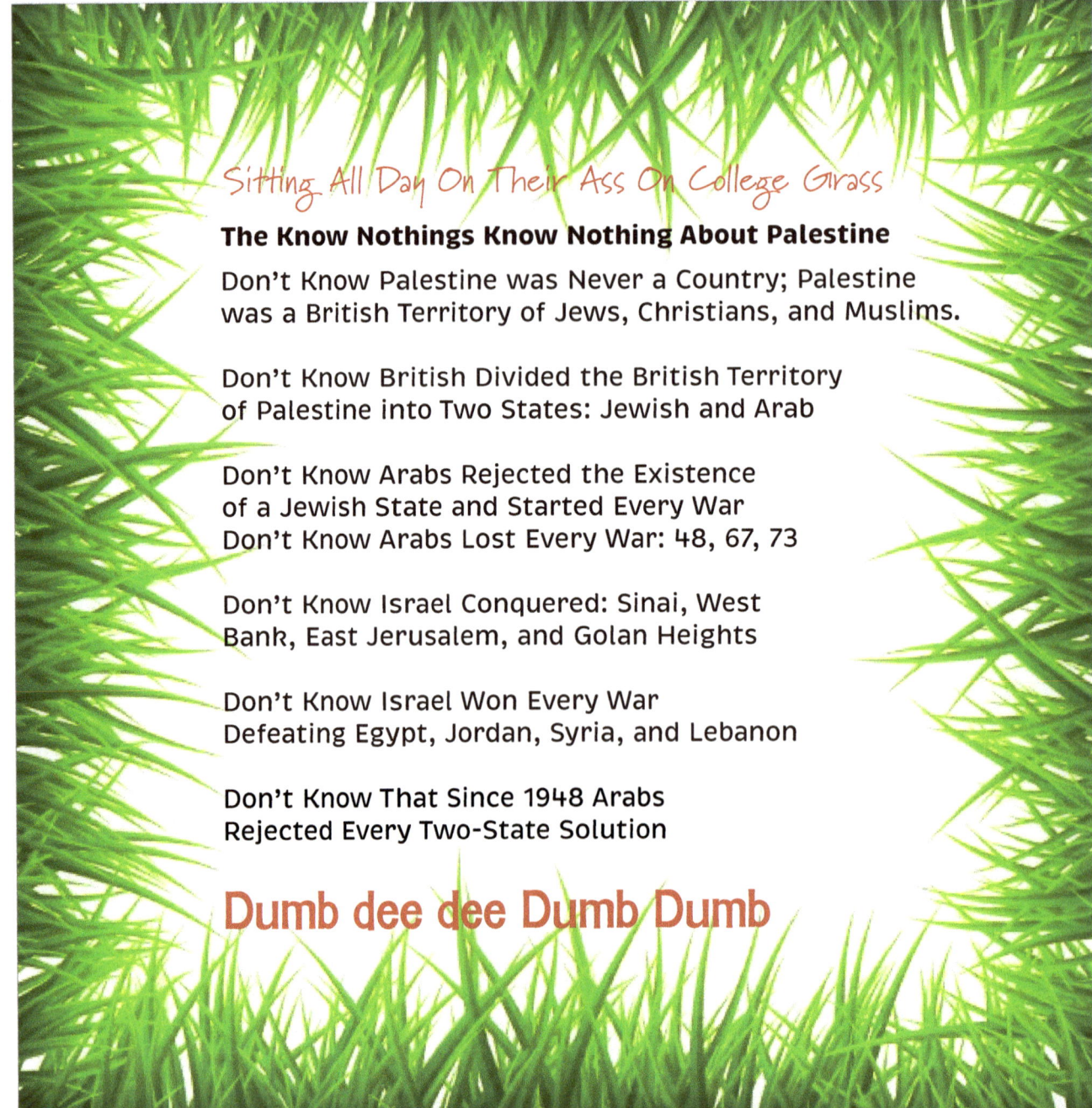

Sitting All Day On Their Ass On College Grass

The Know Nothings Know Nothing About Palestine

Don't Know Palestine was Never a Country; Palestine was a British Territory of Jews, Christians, and Muslims.

Don't Know British Divided the British Territory of Palestine into Two States: Jewish and Arab

Don't Know Arabs Rejected the Existence of a Jewish State and Started Every War
Don't Know Arabs Lost Every War: 48, 67, 73

Don't Know Israel Conquered: Sinai, West Bank, East Jerusalem, and Golan Heights

Don't Know Israel Won Every War Defeating Egypt, Jordan, Syria, and Lebanon

Don't Know That Since 1948 Arabs Rejected Every Two-State Solution

Dumb dee dee Dumb Dumb

Centuries of Islamic Jihad Holy Wars "Allahu Akbar"

Flunked History: Sitting All Day On Their Ass on College Grass

Sitting All Day On Their Ass On College Grass

The Know Nothings Know Nothing About West Bank

Don't Know Jews are the Indiginous Inhabitants of the West Bank: Judea and Sameria

Don't Know That West Bank and Gaza Strip Are Ruled by Warring Terrrorist Gangs: Fatah, Islamic Jihad, Al-Aqsa Martyrs Brigades, Hamas, and Lion's Den

Don't Know Fatah President Abbas Wrote a PhD on Holocaust Denial

Don't Know West Bank Is the Only Place in the World That Celebrates Criminals Released Back into the Neighborhood!

Dumb dee dee Dumb Dumb

Centuries of Islamic Jihad Holy Wars "Allahu Akbar"

Flunked History: Sitting All Day On Their Ass on College Grass

Sitting All Day On Their Ass On College Grass

The Know Nothings Know Nothing About Gaza

Don't Know Samson the Jewish judge traveled to Gaza (Chapters 13-16)

Don't Know Gaza has a 6th Century Synagogue with a Mosaic Floor of King David

Don't Know 4000-Year Gaza Had Many Rulers: Cannaan, Philistine, Rome, Ottoman, British, Egyptian, Israel, Palestinian Authority and Hamas

2007: Don't Know Egypt and Israel Blockade Gaza to Prevent Terrorist Attacks

2007: Don't Know for 18 Years Hamas Turned Gaza into an Underground Tunnel Fortress to Launch 1000's Rockets into Israel

2023: Don't Know Hamas Transformed Gaza into Underground Tunnel Dungeons to Imprison, Torture, Starve, and Rape Hostages

Dumb dee dee Dumb Dumb

Centuries of Islamic Jihad Holy Wars "Allahu Akbar"

Flunked History: Sitting All Day On Their Ass on College Grass

Sitting All Day On Their Ass On College Grass

The Know Nothings Know Nothing About October 7TH

Don't Know Oct 7 Is the Darkest Day in Human History
Don't Know Entire World Is Held Hostage by Hamas

Don't Know Hamas Turned Homes into Flesh-Burning Crematoriums: Ashes Defy Identification

Don't Know Hamas Raped, Murdered, Mutilated and Beheaded Israeli Women at a Dance Festival: "**We Will Dance Again!**"

Don't Know Hamas Beheaded a Soldier to Sell Head to Hamas and IDF Rescued Head

Don't Know Orphaned Holocaust Survivors Are Raising Their Orphaned Grandchildren

Dumb dee dee Dumb Dumb

Centuries of Islamic Jihad Holy Wars "Allahu Akbar"

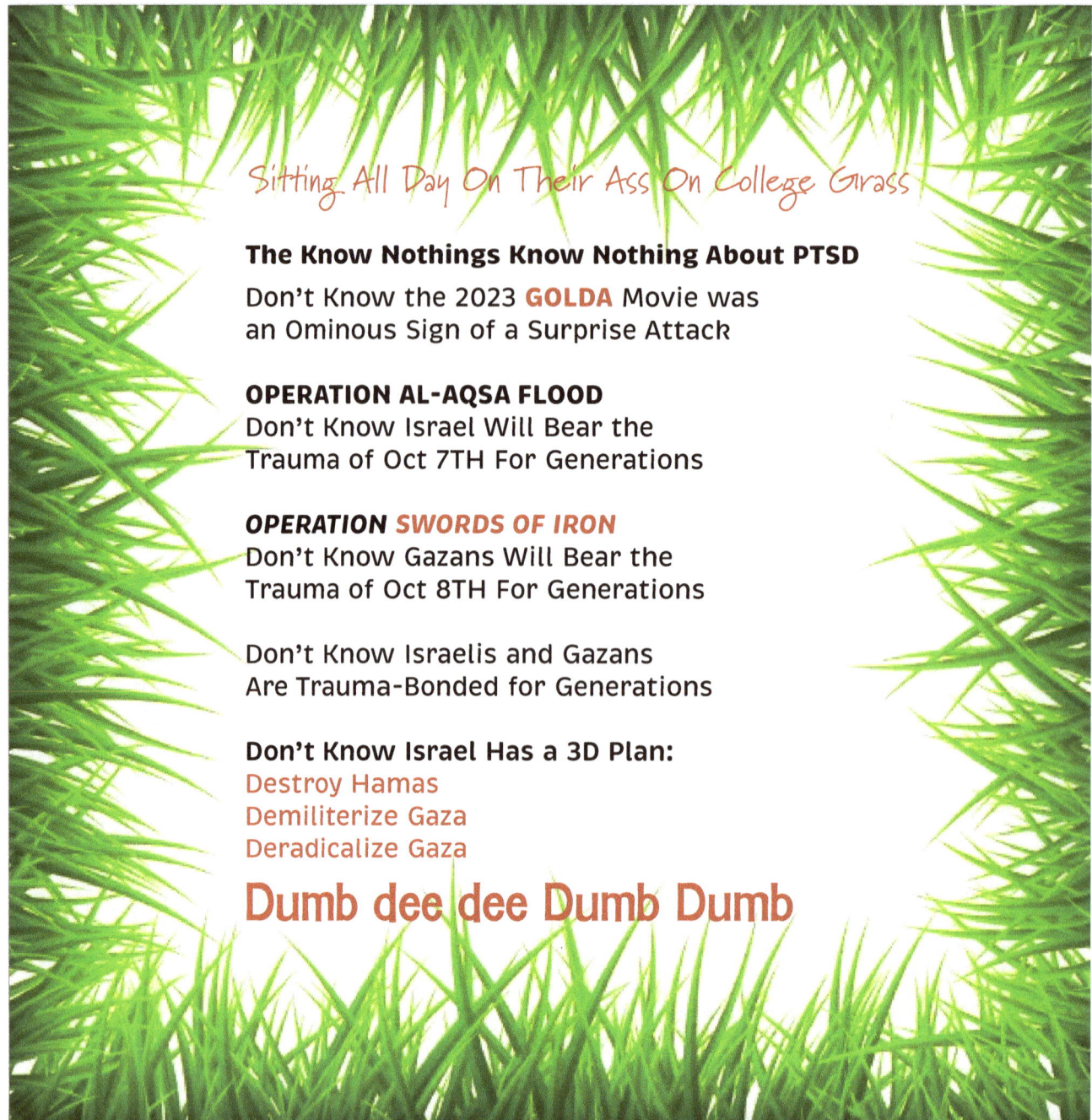

Flunked History: Sitting All Day On Their Ass on College Grass

Sitting All Day On Their Ass On College Grass

The Know Nothings Know Nothing About Palestinain Civilians and Hamas Terrorists

Don't Know There Is No Difference
Hamas Terrorists Are Palestinians

Don't Know Palestinian Children
are Indoctrinated to Hate Jews

Don't Know Hamas will Perpetuate
Terrorist Atrocities Over and Over Again!

Don't Know Palestinian Civilians Assaulted
Hostages Paraded Through Gaza Streets

Don't Know Murdered Naked Body of Shani Louk
was Chosen as **"Picture of the Year!"**

Don't Know Murdered Israeli Civilians
were Abducted into Gaza to Sell to Hamas

Dumb dee dee Dumb Dumb

Centuries of Islamic Jihad Holy Wars "Allahu Akbar"

Flunked History: Sitting All Day On Their Ass on College Grass

Sitting All Day On Their Ass On College Grass
The Know Nothings Know Nothing About Terror

Don't Know Hamas was Designated a Terrorist Organization – Not Liberators

36 YEARS! Don't Know Hamas Murdered Innocent Civilians for 36 Years

18 YEARS: Don't Know Hamas Fired Rockets into Israel for 18 Years

Don't Know **HAMAS CHARTER** Calls For the Murder of All Jews Everywhere

Don't Know Hamas Starts Wars and Breaks Ceasefires: 2008, 2009, 2012, 2012, 2014, 2021 and 2023

Don't Know Hamas Murders Palestinians Who Collaborate with Israel

Don't Know When Hamas Surrenders and Releases Hostages, There Will Be a CEASEFIRE

Dumb dee dee Dumb Dumb

Centuries of Islamic Jihad Holy Wars "Allahu Akbar"

Flunked History: Sitting All Day On Their Ass on College Grass

Sitting All Day On Their Ass On College Grass

The Know Nothings Know Nothing About Israeli Superheroes:

1. Shoot Down Rockets from 6 Countries
   Iran, Gaza, Lebanon, Yemen, Syria, and Iraq
2. Destroy Hamas in Gaza and West Bank
3. Demiliterize Hamas Underground Fortress

Don't Know **Israeli Prime Minister Benjamin** Netanyahu Is the Greatest World Leader Since the Dawn of History!
GOAT: GREATEST OF ALL TIME
16 Years: Innovation Nation
Semi-Socialist State to Free Market Economy

Don't Know **Israeli Ambassador Gilad Erdan** Is the World's Greatest Ambassador Since the Dawn of History!

Don't Know **Israeli Yoav Gallant** and **Israel Katz** Are the World's Greatest Military Leaders Since the Dawn of History!

Now You Know the Difference Between Sons of Light and Sons of Darkness

Centuries of Islamic Jihad Holy Wars "Allahu Akbar"

Flunked History: Sitting All Day On Their Ass on College Grass

Sitting All Day On Their Ass On College Grass

The Know Nothings Know Nothing About Anti-Semitism

Don't Know Education Cannot Ameliorate Anti-Semitism
Haters Hate the Truth, the Facts, and the Light

Don't Know Israel Has All the Right Friends
Israel Has All the Right Enemies

Don't Know:
Those Who Bless Israel Will Be Blessed
Those Who Curse Israel Will Be Cursed
(Bible: Numbers 24:9)

Don't Know in 2023 That You Can't
Murder Jews and Get Away with It!

Don't Know That When You're Jewish
There Is No Such Thing As Too Much Drama!

Now You Know The Difference Between
Sons of Darkness and Sons of Light

Centuries of Islamic Jihad Holy Wars "Allahu Akbar"

What Happens When You Dress Up Albert Einstein As Marilyn Monroe?
SHARON ESTHER LAMPERT

- Prodigy
- Poet
- Prophet
- Philosopher
- Peacemaker
- Paladin of Education
- **PHOTON SUPERHERO**
- Princess KADIMAH
- Princess & Pea
- Performer: Vocalist
- Player: Jock NYU Varsity B-Ball
- President
- Publisher
- Producer
- Psychobiologist: Rockefeller University
- Piano-Playing Cat
- Phoenix
- **PINUP**

WEBSITES
- SharonEstherLampert.com
- WorldFamousPoems.com
- PoetryJewels.com
- PhilosopherQueen.com
- GodIsGoDo.com
- Schmaltzy.com
- TrueLoveBurnsEternal.com
- SillyLittleBoys.com
- WinAtThin.com
- WritersRunTheWorld.com
- PalmBeachBookPublisher.com
- BooksArePowerful.com
- HappyGrandparenting.com
- WomenHaveAllThePower.com

EDUCATION
- Smartgrades.com
- PhotonSuperHero.com
- EveryDayAnEasyA.com
- BooksNotBombs.com

NYU AWARD for "Multi-Interdisciplinary Studies"

CONTRIBUTIONS TO CIVILIZATION
Scientist, Artist, Educator, Theologian

Published 80+ Books
NYU: Perstare et Praestare

PRODIGY
10 Esoteric Laws of Genius and Creativity
Awesome Art of Alliteration Using One Letter of the Alphabet

PROPHET
GOD IS GO! DO!
22 COMMANDMENTS: A UNIVERSAL MORAL COMPASS

PHYSICIST
LAWS OF INEXTRICABILITY - NEW SCIENTIFIC THEORY!

PSYCHOBIOLOGIST
THE SPERM MANIFESTO: 10 RULES FOR THE ROAD - NEW SCIENTIFIC THEORY!

PHILOSOPHER QUEEN
The Philosophy of Love: ME & WE
The Philosophy of Love: THE DOUBLE WHAMMY
Women Have All The Power But Have Never Learned How to Use It

POET
WORLD POETRY RECORD
120 Words of Rhyme from One Family of Rhyme
#1 Poetry Website for Student Projects
The Greatest Poems Ever Written on Extraordinary World Events
First Woman to Write a Book on 5000 Years of Jewish History in 6 Poetic Refrains

PALADIN OF EDUCATION
SMARTGRADES BRAIN POWER REVOLUTION
8 Goalposts of Education
40 Universal Gold Standards of Education
SCHMALTZY: The First Book of Color-Coded Words
Learn to Read Hebrew in One Hour

PSYCHIATRIST
LOVE YOU MORE THAN YESTERDAY: 14 Relationship Strategies for Happily Ever After
Integration Therapy to Rebuild the Broken Wings of Students
3 Stages of Child Abuse
40 Rules of Manhood

PEACEMAKER
WORLD PEACE EQUATION

PINUP
SEXIEST GENIUS IN HUMAN HISTORY

GENIUS: THE GIFT OF DIVINE REVELATION

MY BOOKS WRITE THEMSELVES

I Am Mortal
MY BOOKS ARE IMMORTAL
Please Handle My Books Gently
My Books Are My Remains

Part 1. Birth of Idea: 2023
Part 2. Format Book: January 2, 2024
Part 3. Publish: January 10, 2025

Also By The Genius - 80+ Books

1. Many Jews Reclaimed God, In 5 Minutes Learn 5000 Years of Jewish History
2. TOHO VAVOHU: SIMCHAT TORAH, October 7, 2023
3. POETRY JEWELS: THE GREATEST POEMS EVER WRITTEN ON EXTRORDINARY JEWISH WORLD EVENTS, #1 Poetry Website for Student Projects
4. 17 HOURS: The First Women in the World in a Tank Battle

Sharon Esther Lampert
SEE THE WORLD THROUGH THE EYES OF A CREATIVE GENIUS
Prodigy, Prophet, Philosopher, Poet, Peacemaker, Paladin of Education, Physicist, Princess

FANS@SharonEstherLampert.com

www.ingramcontent.com/pod-product-compliance
Lightning Source LLC
LaVergne TN
LVHW072123060526
838201LV00068B/4957